Read-About® Geography

Lake Tahoe

By Pam Zollman

Subject Consultant
Geoffrey Schladow, PhD, Director
Tahoe Environmental Research Center
University of California
Davis, California

Reading Consultant
Cecilia Minden-Cupp, PhD
Former Director of the Language and Literacy Program
Harvard Graduate School of Education
Cambridge, Massachusetts

Children's Press®
A Division of Scholastic Inc.
New York   Toronto   London   Auckland   Sydney
Mexico City   New Delhi   Hong Kong
Danbury, Connecticut

Designer: Herman Adler Design
Photo Researcher: Caroline Anderson
The photo on the cover shows the clear waters of Lake Tahoe.

Library of Congress Cataloging-in-Publication Data

Zollman, Pam.
  Lake Tahoe / by Pam Zollman.
    p. cm. — (Rookie read-about geography)
  Includes index.
  ISBN 0-516-25036-1 (lib. bdg.)   0-516-29795-3 (pbk.)
  1. Tahoe, Lake (Calif. and Nev.)—Juvenile literature. I. Title. II. Series.
  F868.T2Z65 2006
  917.94'38—dc22   2005026248

CHILDREN'S PRESS, and ROOKIE READ-ABOUT®,
and associated logos are trademarks and/or registered trademarks
of Scholastic Library Publishing. SCHOLASTIC and associated logos
are trademarks and/or registered trademarks of Scholastic Inc.
3 4 5 6 7 8 9 10 R 15 14 13 12 11 10 09 08   62

Which lake was called Big
Water by the Washo Indians?

It's Lake Tahoe!

Lake Tahoe is the second-deepest lake in the United States. It is on the border of two states. Most of Lake Tahoe is in California. The rest of the lake is in Nevada.

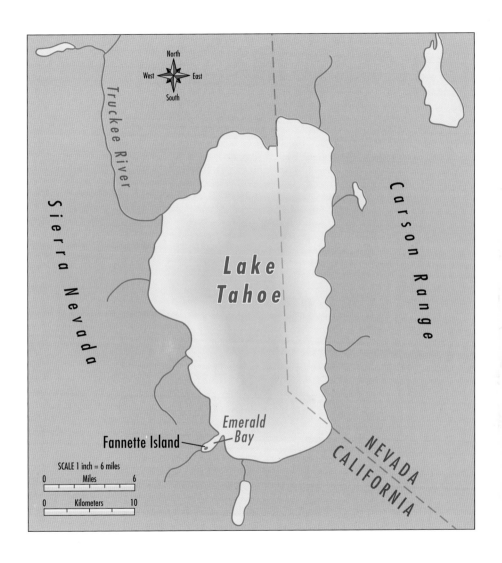

North
West East
South

Truckee River

Sierra Nevada

Carson Range

Lake
Tahoe

Emerald
Bay

Fannette Island

SCALE 1 inch = 6 miles

0 Miles 6

0 Kilometers 10

NEVADA
CALIFORNIA

The Sierra Nevada along Lake Tahoe

Lake Tahoe was formed a long time ago. Huge cracks in Earth's crust, called faults, shifted. They pushed up large blocks of land. These blocks became mountains.

Lake Tahoe is between two mountain ranges. These are the Carson Range and the Sierra Nevada.

Other blocks of land were pushed down. This created a bowl, or basin, in the earth.

Glaciers scraped away at mountains around the basin. A glacier is a slow-moving body of ice. Water from snow, rain, and streams filled the basin. The basin became Lake Tahoe.

Lake Tahoe has clear, blue water. In some spots, you can see 100 feet (30 meters) down into the lake.

Many streams flow into Lake Tahoe. The Truckee River is the only river that flows out of Lake Tahoe.

The Truckee River

Fanny Bridge crosses the Truckee River. People bend over the railing to drop in fish food. They feed the trout that live in the river.

Bass and catfish live in Lake Tahoe.

A bass

Scientists introduced
freshwater salmon to the
lake in 1950.

Fannette Island in Emerald Bay

Emerald Bay is on the south side of Lake Tahoe.

People living in California made Emerald Bay an underwater park. Scuba divers can see sunken boats there.

Fannette Island is Lake Tahoe's only island. Canada geese stay there each spring.

A roadrunner

Quails, wrens, and roadrunners live near Lake Tahoe all year long.

Black bears, mountain sheep, and badgers also make their homes there.

The lake's water temperature stays above freezing in the winter. One of the reasons Lake Tahoe doesn't freeze over is because it is so deep.

Lake Tahoe's winters are cold and filled with snow. Visitors enjoy ice-skating, skiing, and sledding.

Summers are cool at Lake
Tahoe. It rarely rains.
People like to hike, swim,
fish, and play on the beach.

What would you like to do at Lake Tahoe?

Words You Know

Canada geese

Fannette Island

Fanny Bridge

roadrunner

salmon

Truckee River

Index

About the Author

Pam Zollman is an award-winning author of short stories and novels. She is the author of several Rookie Read-About® Geography books. Pam lives in the Pocono Mountains of Pennsylvania and loves Lake Tahoe. She dedicates this book to Eva Perez Byington, who introduced her to the beauty of Lake Tahoe.

Photo Credits

Photographs © 2006: Animals Animals/Earth Scenes/Ben Davidson: 29; Corbis Images: 9 (Joson/zefa), 6 (Galen Rowell), cover, 21, 30 top left (Royalty-Free); Index Stock Imagery: 27 (Kristi Bressert), 10 (David Carriere), 26 (Robert Houser), 22, 31 top left (Larry F. Jernigan), 25 (Richard Stockton); Lonely Planet Images/John Elk III: 3; Masterfile/Garry Black: 18, 30 top right; Photo Researchers, NY: 16 (E.R. Degginger), 23 (Art Wolfe); Robert Winslow: 14, 30 bottom; Seapics.com/Daniel W. Gotshall: 17, 31 top right; Superstock, Inc./Larry Prosor: 13, 31 bottom.

Map by Bob Italiano